The Hollywood Catechism

PRAISE FOR PAUL FERICANO'S POETRY

"A poem is a dangerous weapon in this man's hands."
The Journal of American Poetry

"Should work by Paul Fericano appear someday in *The New Yorker* or *The Atlantic Monthly* it would be a sign that a deal has been made to release the hostages."
The San Francisco Review of Books

"With his own original and distinct brand of humor, Fericano is in the big leagues with writers and satirists such as H. L Mencken, Lenny Bruce, Paul Krassner and Rita Mae Brown."
Gargoyle Magazine

"Fericano is that rare poet who tells the truth with a laugh."
The San Francisco Chronicle

"If a witness protection program for poets existed in this country Fericano would be in it."
Washington Post Book World

"Paul Fericano writes poems like a wanted man hiding out in the basement of *Poetry* magazine."
Chicago Sun-Times

"In the vast literary universe of sober careers and serious awards, it's quite possible that Mssr. Fericano is the "Weird Al" Yankovic of modern poetry."
Littérature Nouvelles (France)

"One of America's best poets."
Ludd's Mill (England)

The Hollywood Catechism

poems

PAUL FERICANO

SILVER BIRCH PRESS
LOS ANGELES, CALIFORNIA

© Copyright 2015, Paul Fericano

Published by Silver Birch Press

ISBN-13: 978-0692384459

ISBN-10: 0692384456

FIRST EDITION: April 2015

EMAIL: silver@silverbirchpress.com

WEB: silverbirchpress.com

BLOG: silverbirchpress.wordpress.com

MAILING ADDRESS:
Silver Birch Press
P.O. Box 29458
Los Angeles, CA 90029

COVER PHOTOGRAPH: Burt Lancaster, *Elmer Gantry* (United Artists, 1960). (Publisher's collection)

for my daughter, Kate

TABLE OF CONTENTS

1. THE BOOK OF SHEMP

The Hollywood Catechism

1. The Book of Shemp

THE ACTOR'S CREED

I believe in Brando,
the Godfather of enormous weight,
creator of mumbling and angst,
and in James Dean, his only ward, our Jim,
who was sold into celluloid by Jack Warner,
born of the hustler Strasberg,
suffered under Rock Hudson,
was speeding, died, and nominated;
descended into gossip hell;
and on his third film was chosen
again from the dead;
ascended into *Giant* heaven,
and is seated in a bathhouse with Brando
the Godfather of enormous weight;
from where he will come to judge
all performances.

I believe in the Holy Spielberg,
the holy casting couch,
the communion of press agents,
the forgiveness of Sally Field,
the resurrection of my career,
and life everlasting without Tom Hanks.
Amen.

The director yells *Cut!* and everyone on the set
is relieved to feel the weight of the day lifted
like a dark comedy of unscripted errors,
no one more thankful than Curly Howard
who retreats to his trailer for a quick smoke and a drink,
rubbing as he goes his shaved cue ball head,
where once the hair grew so thick
he actually appeared handsome to women
who fought to run their fingers through it.

He's reminded now of the sacrifices he's made,
the punishment he endures at the onscreen hands
of his older brother, Moe, who lovingly calls him Babe,
the mixed emotions he feels with each conk on the head,
each slap of the face or fingers poked in bewildered eyes,
and all the bricks and bottles and picks and shovels
and falling pianos and entire buildings collapsing
down around him in heaps of lowbrow humor and pain
can't hide the desperation of his clownish art,
the dreary midnight in his laughter.

Sitting alone, the alcohol convinces him otherwise
and he imagines himself a student of serious literature,
finding wisdom in the works of Edgar Allan Poe,
reading tales of unspeakable horrors befalling others,
grateful for this small refuge of scholarly insight,
and he commits to memory poems of young love dying,
mourning loss in a small room, much like this one,
childlike and powerless to rescue the slipping away,
the black doom of wings waiting above the door,
and he reads as he rocks, repeats the line
Quoth the raven, 'Nevermoe,' over and over again,
until he knows it to be absolutely true.

DEAN MARTIN TALKS
ABOUT WHAT'S BOTHERING HIM

When the moon hit my eye
it had nothing to do with love at all.
For Christ's sake, what was I? A jukebox?

It was like a right-cross-left-hook
combination that I never saw coming.
I deserved it. I danced a little
showed some fancy footwork

but after the first round why bother?
I dropped my guard completely.
I staggered along
until I found the nerve to swagger.

When my voice buckled
under the weight of my own jokes
I went down like the drunk I pretended to be.

After that whenever the moon
took a swipe at me I learned to duck.
I got so good I could make out
and make the bed at the same time.

Not so with those other chumps.
We were all paying our dues in those days.
It was a living.
You sang what they told you to sing.

Some guys believed their own press.
They'd shoot themselves in the head
and expect someone else to drop dead.

Perry Como dreamt of Carolina moons
so often he sleepwalked
through most of the twentieth century.

Andy Williams kept drowning himself
in a moon river no wider than his own smile.

Bing Crosby.
There's a broken record if I ever heard one.
Moonlight becomes you don't make me laugh.

And then there was Frank
the biggest sap of them all.
He flew himself to the moon so many times
he grew wings on his *Gucci's*.

Sure. Half the time
I couldn't sing myself out of an empty casino.
But people got their nickel's worth.
At least I showed up.

All this talk about the moon this and the moon that
and the moon, the moon, the moon.
Let me tell you something: I hate pizza.

FIRST DATE:
THREE QUESTIONS A SENSITIVE MAN ASKS HIMSELF
BEFORE GOING TO SEE A MOVIE

1. Are there two or more women in it who have names?

2. Do they talk to each other?

3. Can I get laid?

LAST DATE:
THREE QUESTIONS A WISE WOMAN ASKS HERSELF
BEFORE GOING TO SEE A MOVIE

1. Are there two or more men in it who have guns?

2. Do they shoot at each other?

3. Where's my pepper spray?

the bartender is talking about ties
and how the color of a tie is directly linked
to a man's sexual attitude

he read it in the "Behavior" section
of *Time* magazine
and he has everyone's ear on this one

"to begin with," he explains
"a blue tie means you're romantic
a red tie means you're passionate
and a green tie means you're macho"

nobody in the place
has ever heard of this color-code

"how about a black tie?" someone asks
"disciplined" he says
"and a white tie?" someone else asks
"selfish" he says

now we really start to get into it

"what about a striped tie?"
"mechanical" he says
"checkered?"
"god-like"
"spotted?"
"reckless"
"bow?"
"abusive"
"string?"
"extremely depraved"

"this doesn't say much" i say
"for those of us who never wear a tie"

suddenly, all of us are aware
that I'm the only one in the place
who is actually wearing a tie
and it's an ascot

somebody finally breaks the silence:
"what about shoes?"

CHICO MARX EXPLAINS OPERA

Sure, I listen to opera.
I watch opera all the time on TV.
She's got a magazine, too.
But I don't read so good.

A Direct Correlation
Between the War on Terror
And the Proliferation
Of Penis Enlargement Spam

Seek immediate medical help
if your erection lasts longer than 100 years.

I'm at the Academy Awards ceremony
sitting at a table
with Edgar Allan Poe, Walt Whitman
and Mrs. McBain, my fifth grade teacher
who starts writing on my dinner napkin in red ink:
Read more . . .

When I hear my name announced
as the winner of that year's *Best Supporting Poet*
and find myself being pushed out in the aisle
running towards the stage
and passing Leonard Nimoy
who's shaking everyone's hand for me.

When I finally reach the podium
to accept my Oscar from Rod McKuen,
Allen Ginsberg suddenly rushes out
from behind a curtain
grabs my Oscar
thanks a bewildered audience
and then races out a side door
where Lawrence Ferlinghetti is waiting
in a tan Ford Galaxy
with New York plates.

When I return to my table
everyone tries their best to console me.

Poe says that ee cummings
pulled the same stunt on T.S. Eliot years ago
diving through a closed window
and falling into an alley
where Wallace Stevens waited in a Chevy van.

Whitman says he knows a place around the corner
where we can all get a sausage sandwich
and a whiskey
and meet some guy
who claims to be Carl Sandburg in drag.

And Mrs. McBain
finishes writing on my dinner napkin in red ink:
Read more Emily Dickinson

HOLY COW IT'S MOSES

not really

it's just your strong
American memory
of all things Charlton Heston
commanding a reverent hush
in your Hollywood dream

listen:
one nation under God
indivisible like the Red Sea

I DON'T CARE IF I NEVER GET BACK

The home team is up
and I sit in the upper deck seats
far to the right of home plate
high up and down the line
binoculars around my neck
glove in hand.

It's my first visit
to Candlestick Park
the new home
of the San Francisco Giants
since moving west
from New York in 1959.

I lean forward in anticipation
slap my glove
and all the old timers smile.
A foul ball this far out
this far up in the nosebleed section
is as rare and dizzy
as the air is thin.

I allow myself
the pleasure of tall daydreams
standing on the peak of distraction
where everything soars
so close to sky:

a one-legged man
in front of me
drinking from two cups of beer
a boy across the aisle
in leg braces
dressed like *Superman*
a woman in a pink sun hat
who looks like Ethel Merman.

My father sits next to me,
a *Camel* cigarette
dangling from his lips
the nimble fingers
of his calloused hands
cracking peanuts
dropping empty shells
on his *Teamster* boots.

I stare through the lenses
at orange light towers
high above the stadium
study a small catwalk
until I am there
higher up
a fearless David in a house
of fearsome Goliaths.

I cast my eyes downward now
to the batter's box
and a big beautiful black
and white speck
of a giant ballplayer
kicks the dirt and digs in.

A miniature of his true self
a tiny baseball card figure
swinging a bat
in the centerfield of my thoughts.

I fumble with the focus
and try to bring him into view.

But he turns his back
just as the number 24 explodes
off his jersey.

Far below
my father's voice beckons me
calls me back down.

I hear the words:
"Willie Mays is up, son,"
and I slap my glove.

THE THREE STOOGES
MEET CHARLES BUKOWSKI IN HEAVEN

The day is like any other day in Paradise
where angels hang out on street corners in between gigs

smoking filtered cigarettes drinking ginger ale
and swapping stories about the Son of Man.

Everyone has an eye fixed on Jesus.
He's on his knees in an alley shooting dice

with the Three Stooges
and the poor bastards are losing their shirts.

The Savior of the World is on fire.
In flowing red robe he rattles the bones in his hand

brings them to his ear shakes them like the Second Coming
and blows on them once for luck.

He arcs his fist before release and shouts:
Baby needs a new pair of shoes!

then tosses them with the same force his father summoned
to create the Milky Way.

When he flashes that wide resurrection smile
the one he showed the Romans right before they nailed him,

he scoops up his winnings with a wink and a nod
and everyone knows the Lamb of God is on a roll.

The Stooges are victims of divine intervention.
They make the sign of the cross and Jesus smiles.

I like you guys, he says, slapping their faces affectionately.
And just like that three morons become saints.

Leaning against a wall drinking beer from a bottle
always cold never empty is Charles Bukowski.

He shifts his weight like a man itching to start something
eyeing the action as if he's writing his last poem.

Jesus stands now and introduces them.
The Stooges pull back unsure of what to expect from a guy

who once threw up on Norman Mailer and just last week
tried to look up the Virgin Mary's dress.

Bukowski hesitates, too. He remembers almost losing an eye
in a pie fight and watches their fingers closely now

the air so choked with mistrust even the Holy Ghost is scared.
That's when Jesus stands on his head.

It's a minor miracle, not like changing a Beatles' song
into a jingle for running shoes, but it breaks the tension at last.

Sighs of relief rise up like hosannas and everyone laughs,
especially the Son of God who isn't wearing underpants.

Thank You Elizabeth Taylor

for surviving the Hollywood
under your nails
all those Eddie Fisher records
skipping in your head
the Richard Burton years
echoing in your best screams
the uncorked bottles
the pills by the nightstand
the excessive weight
the plastic surgery
the heavy makeup
the chicken bone in your throat
thank you for not dying
for not being destroyed
by those two Oscars
a comedian's joke
your husband's campaign lies
and for telling the world
that Laurence Harvey
was your dearest friend
when nobody else could stand him

thank you for making distinctions
for not committing suicide
when everyone was writing poems
to a dead Marilyn Monroe

The more celebrated *Common Dullard*
is a frequent visitor year-round
and is often indistinguishable

From the *Great Dolt*
or the *Lesser Dimwit*
or even the *Least Clodpate* of the species.

The call of each are difficult to tell apart:
a relentless chirping for attention
an incessant squawking for no reason
a persistent quacking for itself.

Exercise caution in the wild.
Avoid contact during mating season.
Look for splotches near the rump.

Field glasses are helpful when used incorrectly.

GROUCHO MARX
THROWS OUT THE FIRST PITCH

As the familiar strains of *Tosca*
repeat themselves tonight,
take a bicarbonate of soda
and skip the first act entirely.

If you can't skip, try prancing.

All in all we feel certain
you'll be thrilled and delighted
by Puccini's music,
which should come as surprise
since we're actually presenting
Verdi's *La traviata* instead.

Of course, for the second act
we hope to revive Rossini
if we can sober him up and find out
what he did with Mussorgsky.

We tried to locate Handel
but all we found was a brass doorknocker.

And if Rossini can't play
we've got Donizetti ondeck to pinch hit,
although it isn't likely he'll get on base
with Tinkers, Evers and Chance
roaming the orchestra pit.

Nevertheless, we have a strong lineup
with Stravinsky on the mound,
Offenbach and Bizet in the outfield
and Wagner batting cleanup
and doing the dishes.

In fact, we've got a pretty good chance
of winning the pennant this year
if we can just stay away from the third act.

It would have been
a different opera season altogether
if we could have signed DiMaggio.

THE HALLE BERRY

Halle Berry,
fool of none,
the Oscar is with thee.
Blessed art thou among catwomen,
and blessed is the fruit
of thy loom, *Jockey*.

Holy Berry,
mother of Chuck,
root for us winners
now and at the hour
of our last stand.
X-men.

I

Among twenty armed policemen,
The only moving thing
Was the eye of the black man.

II

I was of three opinions,
Like a newscast
In which there are three black men.

III

The black man sailed in the tenement winds.
He was a small part of the sidewalk.

IV

A job and a chance
Are one.
A job and a chance and a black man
Are wondering.

V

I do not know which to consider,
The ugliness of inquiries
Or the ugliness of identities,
The black man reaching for his wallet
Or just after.

VI

Indecision filled the windshield
With broken glass.
The beating of the black man
Crossed it, back and forth.
The blood
Traced in the beating
An illegible scrawl.

VII

O fat boys of Sanford,
Why do you imagine a pure race of men?
Do you not see how the black man
dies at the feet
Of the children about you?

VIII

I know ignoble allegations
And rude, inexhaustible change;
But I know, too,
That the black man is not concerned
With what I know.

IX

When the black man marched in plain sight,
He marked the start
Of one of many endings.

X

At the sight of black men
slumping in a circular red light,
Even the dregs of cacophony
Would wail and shake their heads.

XI

He descended on Florida
In a bulletproof train.
Once, a confidence deserted him,
In that he confused
The roar of his engines,
For black men.

XII

The land is moving.
The black man must be singing.

XIII

It was night all morning.
It was hailing
And it was going to hail.
The black man sat
on the pitched-roof.

it's just not enough
it's not enough of Elvis whiskey decanters
Elvis toilet paper
Elvis condoms
Elvis impersonators singing Elvis songs
to Elvis fans
Elvis albums pitched on Elvis TV sets
to Elvis moonies
Elvis Cadillacs that travel Elvis highways
Elvis socks that fill Elvis shoes
Elvis snow skis with matching Elvis parkas
Elvis pillboxes stuffed with Elvis drugs
for Christ's sake it's just not enough
not enough of Elvis handguns
good-luck stick pins
disposable douche bags
golf balls
garage door openers
hideaway beds
and even poems like this that make you tired
it's not enough of Elvis
it's just not enough

we dig up the grave
and sell little envelopes of Elvis plots
we pulverize the casket
and market little vials of Elvis coffins
we auction off the corpse
and sell every last bone to the highest bidder
there's an Elvis foot
there's an Elvis foot without the Elvis toes
an Elvis collarbone
an Elvis spine jawbone ribcage finger
an Elvis thumb with part of an Elvis thumbnail
and of course there's an Elvis pelvis
fetching the highest price in modern history
for a single work of art
and still it's not enough of Elvis
it's just not enough
we don't have enough
we can't get enough
and we won't rest until we've had enough

Moe stands at one end of the counter
puffing on a pipe full of *Prince Albert*

blowing smoke rings
big enough to drive his *Studebaker* through.

Freud stands at the other end
puffing on a giant *Corona-Corona*

watching the smoke spin above his head
like a recurring dream.

This is not a place for talking or joking.
It's a place for quiet smoldering

where the cloud between the two men
is as thick as a couch, as thin as a gag.

Freud plays with his cigar now.
He strokes it, rolls it, turns it over,

slides it slowly between his fingers
then shoots Moe a knowing glance.

Moe stares past him with comic eyes
searching his slapstick brain

for one devastating wisecrack
that can drip from his lips like sap.

Instead, he says nothing.
He just puffs on his pipe and winks at Freud.

Freud pretends it's all in good fun
but moves away from the counter, just in case.

THE DIRECTOR'S PRAYER

Our Fellini
who Art in Carney,
Clooney be thy name.
Thy King be Kong,
thy Penn be Sean,
in Bert as it is in Ernie.

Give us our way
with Doris Day,
and forgive us
our Joan Crawfords,
as we forgive Eddie
for leaving Debbie,
and lead us not
into Snake Canyon,
but deliver us from Evel
Knievel.

Cut.

I.

It's November 22, 1955, the morning
of his own demise. Shemp Howard staggers
through the streets of Burbank, California,
looking for his kid brother, Curly.

He's been up all night
in every bar from here to San Gabriel.
He tries to remember where he parked his car.
Then he remembers he doesn't own a car.

He doesn't even have a driver's license.
He considers calling his brother Moe
but changes his mind.
He'll talk to him tonight after the fights.

II.

It's late May, 1946.
Shemp shows up early on the Columbia lot,
his first day replacing Curly who is ill.
He jokes with the crew until brother

Moe arrives.
They go over a script change with the director.
Shemp is reluctant to fill in but he knows
Moe and Larry will be out of a job if he doesn't.

A contract with Harry Cohn
is like the kiss of death.
It's not forever, he tells himself:
Curly will be back before I can say ebebebe.

III.

The light from the lamp by his bed illuminates
the characters on the page
until the faces of Tom and Huck
become as real as his own imagination.

While sitting in makeup,
Shemp talks about the dream
he had last night. He and Curly are sitting
in the backseat of a speeding car.

Nobody is driving. Both light up cigars.
Curly says: *Don't look now*
but I think we're about to be killed.
Shemp laughs so hard he wakes himself up.

IV.

There's a certain feel
to the Hollywood in his bones every time
he walks down a sidewalk and brushes up
against the fame of all that other stuff.

Curly appears on the set
for the first time since his stroke.
He's let his hair grow and lost some weight.
The spark is still there so they use him

in a brief cameo.
It's the first time all three
Howard brothers appear onscreen together.
Shemp kids his baby brother and pinches his cheeks.

V.

There are hundreds of stories
no one will hear. He's okay with that.
He's already forgotten most of the punch lines
to some of his favorite jokes.

Shemp is devoted to his wife.
He calls her *Babe.* When they first meet
she's in the chorus of a vaudeville show.
One night he does his act onstage

and takes a punch from another comic
that splits his lip and knocks him out cold.
When he finally comes to
he's resting in the arms of an angel.

VI

When he can't pay
his electric bill he lives in the dark
for two months. Candles don't help. He's evicted
after setting fire to the bedroom curtains.

In 1939, Shemp is a well dressed
man about town. He has a successful solo film
career and the studio bills him
as "The Ugliest Man in Hollywood."

He plays along with the gag.
He goes home at night and pours a drink.
Deep cuts don't show where the laughs
keep coming no matter what he does.

VII

When he's with friends
he's easily distracted by a dog's bark.
It strays into his brain
like the sound of a trumpet no one else hears.

Shemp leaves the set early
to do his Christmas shopping at Bullock's.
He stops and stares in the window
at the toy train that circles around a tiny

mountain village. *Where does it go, kid?*
He says this aloud to his only son,
Mort, who is twenty years old and on a train
coming home from college.

POEM FOR RALPH EDWARDS

This is your poem.

FATHER WRITES TO ANN LANDERS
AND LOOKS FOR PRACTICAL GUIDANCE

November 11, 1961

What message is a boy sending
when sometimes he lets himself be kissed
and sometimes he doesn't?

There's this boy I really like.
We've been together a few times
including an overnight outing
with our local church group.

The problem is I can't tell
if he cares for me
the same way I care for him.

I don't know if he's being friendly
or just pretending.
Sometimes he acts excited
and other times
he just sits there doing nothing.

Once he said my breath smelled
which really hurt my feelings.

I heard someone once say
that if you want a boy to like you
buy him things he likes.

This boy likes football.
So I bought him a football and a helmet
and lots of packs of football cards.

For awhile he was cooperative.
We'd play catch and he'd let me hug him
when we were alone.

He'd sit on the floor in my room
and sort through all the cards
while I played with his hair.

But lately all he ever wants to do is chew
that awful gum that comes with the cards
and talk about Johnny Unitas.

He won't let me kiss him anymore.
He pulls away from me
no matter how hard I try to please him.
.

I have a terrible fear
he wants to be left alone
and that I'll never see him again.

I'm losing confidence in myself.
Today he actually ran the other way
when he saw me coming.

I don't know what to do.
How do I get a boy to like me?
How do I get a boy to care?

And who is Johnny Unitas?

AND LANDERS WRITES BACK TO FATHER
AND PUNTS THE BALL

November 27, 1961

Johnny Unitas
is the quarterback for the Baltimore Colts.

THE OTHER MAN AS TRANSLATOR

No matter how calmly a woman speaks:
I need you to tell me what you're feeling.

Or how sympathetic she tries to be:
Do you understand what I'm trying to say?

A man won't hear what a woman is saying:
I don't know what you're talking about.

Until her words come from the mouth of another man:
What the fuck is wrong with you?

Another man who is strong but sensitive:
Try to stay focused, pal.

Creating a false sense of bravado in the man:
Hey, asshole, stay out of this.

Compelling the other man to take control:
Who are you calling asshole, you deaf motherfucker?

Causing the man to reconsider his position.
I feel sick to my stomach.

Prompting the other man to challenge his beliefs:
Grow the fuck up.

Allowing the woman to step back in:
No, no. That's a good start.

And permitting the other man to validate the process:
Oh, yeah. Right.

Like right speech, it should be practiced with restraint,
usually, when you don't have anything helpful to say,

about children, opera, or anything else for that matter.
And besides, no one asked for your opinion, anyway.

A Beautiful Day in the Neighborhood

I sit in a chair next to my friend's empty plastic pool
drinking and discussing the relationship of poetry
to the Epic of Gilgamesh and the Vedic texts

and the cartoon violence of Laurel & Hardy,
two of the most underrated mob influences
of any post modern literary crime wave.

The cold beer and warm tequila scorch my thoughts
while slapstick theories sizzle like steaks
on my friend's Fourth of July barbeque.

I argue that Babylonian verse and Sanskrit literature
and the milking of a gag can all be used in poetic service
to complement the absurd nature of reality.

As my eyelids grow heavy and my face drops away
I adjust my sunglasses and pretend to see
what Steve McQueen saw when he looked in a mirror.

My friend is a big quiet drinker from Oklahoma.
He listens to me intently as if a coyote is calling him back
to where the corn is as high as an elephant's eye.

He drains his long neck bottle of genuine draft
and savors the last vanishing drop of *Miller Time*.
Then he looks through the bottle as if it's a telescope.

"No matter how hard you try," he says
"you can't stop two lunatics from busting up your yard
and scaring your chickens to death."

I'm startled. My friend is not always so philosophical.
I start to disagree but have trouble slurring my hypothesis.

"That's their job," he helps clarify for me,
as if he's just explained gravity to a three year old.

I squint now. I can barely make him out as he shifts
and changes shape and begins to resemble
someone in sneakers and a zippered cardigan.

I'm the first to admit I drink too much.
But nobody makes more sense than Mister Rogers.

THE GUN CONTROL INTELLIGENCE TEST

This is your lock and load lifetime warranty.
This is your foolproof beer chaser.

This is your stuffed and mounted Trigger.
This is your camouflaged finger.

This is your tire swing in the gorilla cage.
This is your Planet Gorski.

This is your shiny new dunce cap.
This is your same old head.

What don't you understand about this poem?

In the name of the Bogart,
and of the Cagney,
and of the Holy Edward G.
Amen, see?

2. Howl of Lon Chaney, Jr.

HOWL OF LON CHANEY, JR.

For Larry Talbot

I.

I heard the best lines of my creation butchered by pretenders,
      slap-dashed mangled stepped on,
screeching themselves through the tortured takes at night
      looking for an absent cue,
improvised words with phony accents in forgotten films
      chewing scenery cold print on unfinished scripts
      scribbled on distressed pages
defamed by rank producers, third-rate moguls, two-bit hams
      with unfiltered burns on yak-hair fingers waiting for
      that quick take sound stage opening night premiere,
who stumped and pumped the ballyhoo press that wailed
      the ghost sound clickety-clack of lead type on
      rolled paper ruminating box office hit,
who punctured dreams of pure-hearted men who said their
      prayers by night becoming wolves when wolfbane
      bloomed and moons were full and bright,
who pimped for stand in movie fathers swinging silver-headed
      walking sticks that bashed the skulls of
      sacrificial sons onscreen,
who searched the painted backdrop skies for costars,
      telescopic hindsight peering into deconstructed movie
      sets where chance encounters go to die,
who stitched together green hide stiffs with stolen body parts
      and square-shaped heads electrified in hunchback storms,
who sucked the bloodline in studio castles or drank all night in
      vampire curses, stench, or cement spliced their
      bit parts the morning after
with daylight spools, with dupes, with double exposures,
      Cinema-scope and music scores and endless riffs,
incredibly dumb, halls of withering makeup men and
      hazing in the brain slipping pools of Frances and
      Oklahoma, obscuring all the whirlwinds of mother within,
Alcohol vagaries of planks, bedroom dirt dark carpeted nights,
      boozy recollections under the steps, catfight alleys of
      doughboy runs crayon smearing flashlight, cop and gun
      and billy club in the menacing foil of Los Angeles
      dumpster duty and dull blur dissolve of film,
who filled the milk lungs of terrified moviegoers choking back
      the horror of soda-pop screams, until the whine of
      camera screws and cranks crushed them into sniveling
      simpering lunatics and barren of grey matter all

shortchanged of brilliance on the cutting room flatbed
       of continuity,
who robbed each chance for fame with silver bullets shot
       from rented sequels fired by payroll hacks,
who tortured any thought of a comeback, navigate,
       switchback trails high above the poorly lit set,
       piecemeal mind, dim, cloistered like a monkey
       on their back,
maimed the chance of being named to any best dressed list,
       opportunities squandered, wasted in brown derby
       booths, hands in sidewalk cement jackhammered
presto chango smoke and mirrors, breaking the fourth wall
       spilling their guts like a photo shoot
       grinning aspect-ratio images on the screen
begging the bald-faced bigwigs to sign checks for two-bit
       parts in B movies with cheap careers guaranteed
       to leak the small print on blotted contracts,
       who vanished into aerial shot bottles of empty Jack
       highball, quick-change artist they ached for,
suffering the cringes and furrows of neglect abandoned
       apple box, half apple in backlot towns, messages pinned
       to dressing room doors knocking and knocking still,
who calculated profits created with miniatures, two timing
       slide rules backwind barney blankets covering both sides
       of no way out, cold sweat convincers swimming in
       drunk tank emulsions
who lit coronas for studio fat cats in flimflam suits of
       imported guff and couldn't tell the difference between
       the horror and the horrible if it bit them on the neck.
who studied Hull Benicio Landon Peter Stubbe of the Wheel
       Cinema and synchronized machines because the film
       invariably unwound at their feet in Bedburg,
who slouched behind the scenes in mummy makeup beseeching
       uninspired gofer demons who were uninspired gofer
       demons,
who knew they were nearly sane when Berserkers
       tracked in ghostlike agony,
who chased after gypsies in caravans with vikacis in Latvia
       on the verge of full moon shadow road with index
       and middle finger the same length,
who hunted ravenous and friendless through Westwood
       looking for iron or steel or raw meat, and read the
       bloodstain trades to learn about Hollywood hereafter,
       a noble gesture, and so took lip to bootleg liquor,
who followed into movie theaters of double features trailing
       behind everything with tail of red palm hair
       and the thick and thin of lines howled in free verse

speech Burbank,
who resurfaced on the beach at San Clemente engaging the
      N.R.A in mustache and overcoats with small forked
      tongues screaming in their diffident obsession,
      their excuse for not learning their lines,
who chopped off their ears with bread knives declaring
      themselves cancer free of the studio system,
who peddled plastic classic monster models in Aurora
      big time money dripping creeps while the kids
      in comic book towns traded body parts painted
      day glow, and glue fixed themselves high in Woolworth
      stores, as all America inhaled,
who showed up retching in drug store parking lots with
      two cases of beer shaking before the ice machine with
      future fans,
who clawed directors in the face and spit with fear
      in dressing rooms for breaking no silence but their
      own dead talk animal humping and debauchery,
who yowled on their haunches in the trailers and were
      drugged into whiskey soda clutching rewrites and bare
      buttocks palm hair wild and red
who let their guts be ripped apart by pimping publicity
      pushers, and thanked them with interest,
who ravaged and were ravaged by fathers who spoke of
      mothers being dead for years, rotating circular pan
      360 degrees around their own fixed axis,
who drank in the morning in the evenings in side
      door entrance stairwells and the dark theater lobbies
      graveyard leaking their guts religiously to
      compensate for the sake of compensation,
who practice sorcery behind the downfall making pacts
      with devils, such warm blood from veins
      in search of prey, actual or perceived movement
      camera tilted, imbalance, transition, hoarse raspy,
      heavy with drink and smoke and instability,
who misplaced their parents to the three old bastards of luck
      the one armed bastard of the final cut
      the one armed bastard that shakes down the deal
      and the one armed bastard who gets everything
      he can out of them before 1 pm because
      after that they can't guarantee anything,
who mated dark shadows of ignorance and superstition with
      frequent and atrocious attacks half-eaten
      son of silent screen submerged in the depths
      of a shocked existence, a half shell of a former life,
who processed changes of colors into various shades of grey
      the hairback shivering moments of age-old cameras

cut, cornered, sharp sticks and spears and dogs
set on them naked in the woods behind their houses,
who filled washtubs with ale packed in ice, Mother Cleva
drinking, swallowing her voice bichloride of mercury
rumors as the hunchback performed on stage
at the Majestic and years believing her dead, stealing
Chiaroscuro, shining Cinerama shown on curved panels,
screaming into close-ups, their faces filling the pilfered
savagery of crimes beyond imagination hiding
in forests, warm blood from veins in search of prey,
young girls playing together, milking cows in the fields,
who fade out in vast fisheye lenses, exposed light increased &
decreased, gradually beginning or ending scenes
appearing and reappearing in shots staring into cameras,
stumbling out of dressing rooms hung over
on whiskey and lies,
who ran all night with their feet bloodied and torn
by rock and stone the riverbeds hiding all trace, all scent,
escaping from the self kept at bay, waiting at the door,
crying wolf too many times and waiting for a window
to open in a soft-lighted room full of warmth
and kindness,
who retreated to the front in great suicidal battles with
arguments and rages and deep cuts in production values
teetering in trucks near cliffs and overdoses on fighting
streets of North Hollywood, yellow headlamp of a full
moon & their voices ripped laughing from their throats,
who pimped for vaudeville comics and fed the beast a putrid stew
of bottom feeders from the remade dregs of Bowery
Boys routines and dead-end shtick,
who snapped the clapboard crane shot mounted on a platform
making their debut at six months in one of their phantom
father's stage shows,
who left school, got married and began a career as boilermakers,
newsboys, icemen, farmhands, metal workers,
clothing salesmen, plumber's helpers, hawking illegal
booze to speakeasies,
who drank alone on the sound stages of Universal City
embalmed in Jim Beam under the delirium sky bombed
and bounded by gin singers and pot preachers,
who sang all night swinging and flinging over kitchen sink
recitations which glowed in the bright red evening
that played out melodies of Gilgamesh,
who ate brains from cracked open skulls feasting on carcasses
burned to ash & powder imagining the innocent
realm of dumb giants named Lennie crushing mice,
who disguised themselves in animal skins and talked

to children in red riding hoods,
who threw themselves off the roofs of castles on closed sets
while mothers washed and cooked on ranches
in the San Fernando Valley
who swallowed forty sleeping pills mistreating retreating
into trucks and rushed to hospitals, forced to act
in horrific films that no one went to see, growing
hair on the palms of their hands,
who were buried alive in their mummified bandaged skins
on Hollywood and Vine after long hours in make-up
chairs & the trumped-up charges & wide-angle dregs
of manipulating producers & the superimposed screams
of the Edge Fog lightleak & the dollygrip of malevolent
dolly shots run out of town by the raving
rough house joy of Count Gamula,
who were born two months premature, dead black, plunged into
icy Belle Isle Lake and shocked back to life like a
B-movie plot this actually happened and survived
in shoebox incubators clinging and holding fast
in the cruel fright night of Oklahoma territory
winter & snow and no cigars passed out,
who cried out blue-skinned without oxygen, barely audible
carpet-laying furniture dealing in between bookings,
serving as props in musical comedy acts from Chicago
to Vancouver to Colorado, westward riding railroad
thespian parents raised and lowered song and dance
on trash strewn stages near-empty orchestra pits
of nickelodeon Americana ragtime whiskey and scotch
puking before curtain in alleys behind theaters angry
voices and the force of a star performance,
who hitchhiked across screen-tests and refused to change
their names until 1935 starved and willing to
pull the inner sanctum over their eyes hard-
drinking boisterous pranks scaring women and
children and giving the men shudders,
who drove themselves mad in the midnight hour to find out
if I had a career or you had a career or he had
a career to find out Academia,
who traveled to Hollywood who died in Hollywood, who
returned to Hollywood & killed time, who
spied on Hollywood & moped & refinanced in
Hollywood and finally left to discover the
Year, & now Hollywood is desperate for her icons,
who ended their careers in low budget spider baby
house of the black death trash pleading for the right
part that morphed attractive stars-to-be into
aging grotesque physical hulks in only 20 years

until the soul begged eternity for release,
who donated their bodies to science and soaked their liver and
lungs and brains in alcohol waiting for curious
medical students with promising futures and the itch
to dissect the demons who spoke their rocking chair
odes to High Noon,
who fled to Arcadia to hunt for easy prey or Cologne
to deliver Zeus or Bedburg to young girls
or Wells Fargo to the pillow of death
or Damascus to Albuquerque to Bandit Island to the
fireball jungle or badlands of South Dakota,
who spoke with hoarse raspy speech impediments in front of
live audiences & were freeze-framed with chronic heart
disease & gaffer's tape masked in circular cave
drawings with hand-held shots & a hangman's noose,
who smoked peace pipes of dark opium with NBC programmers
and sacrificed themselves on imported Italian marble
floors of gossip mongers and rumor peddlers with Yul
Brynner grins shaved clean and regenerating wounds
immune to disease, invoking instant replay cranial
assaults,
and who morphine dripped magnetic Dexedrine hybrid
straitjacket rip-offs for hypno-hep lounge lizards creeping
trick or treat therapy from razor blade candy dingdongs &
insomnia,
who in reckless frenzy in battle fearing no one feeling no pain,
never surrendering with coats of mail for protection,
returning with hair on the inside of their skin, invisible men under
four names for extras stunts bits and leads with no rest,
crossing oceans and roaming the countryside
eastward,
United Kingdom's Wales' Llanwelly's and Talbot Castle's empty
halls, weeping with the shrieks of the Ouspenskaya,
howling and prowling in the full moon villainous
stop-motion transformations of desire, vision
of delusional living, shapeshifting bodies as prehistoric
as unholy ground,
with father finally ******, and the last incredible script
memorized in turrets high behind zoom shots,
and the final wipe and the final cookie board clapped
in response and the final death scene traced in hairlines
snipped from the final threadbare inner dialogue,
heavenly bodies spied on in bedrooms above antique
shops, and even there a life is doomed to fantasy,
a mere game of chance in a world of suggestion—
ah, Larry, while you are not alive I am not alive, and
now you're finally in the celluloid ethereal stew of

60

TCM time—
and who hence returned home after 18 years sitting high atop
  Mt. Wilson with a brilliant curiosity for the dark unknown
  of the greater horizontal plane of action the overlap &
  the trembling heavens,
who memorized and made disconsolate slips in gypsy rhyme bitten
  by Bela and crushed his skull to be typecast and trapped
  by angels of production codes through eye-line match cut
  between two shots and created illusions and separated
  marginal utterances and called forth ancient curses and
  ripped human tongues with wisdom of Suscipiat Dominus
  Sacrificium De Manibus Tuis
to endure the part, six hours of Jack Pierce pasted yak hair and
  stranded kelp T-shaped nosepiece molded rubber fang
  teeth hair palms feet tiptoed into padded paws, the shock
  soundless and dumbfounded and quaking with rejection
  yet professing a soul to play the game to play the scene
  to the movement of silence in this sad and endless role,
the wolfman son and lover hound in timeless stray, bitter,
  yet tasting sweet deep within what might be left to savor
  before the full burn of restored night,
and emerged clad in motion picture robes and radiant age
  of flickering champs and rogues relieving the suffering
  of America's thirst for silver screen escape into
  a carl carl laemmle laemmle faemmle clarion call
  that shook cities down to the last movie palace
with the digital film on the projector of life rewound
  from their own two-reelers good to watch a thousand
  times a thousand years over.

II.

What conglomerate of muscle and means laid waste
  their skills and pimped their talent and creativity?
Universal! Power! Control! Horror! Iron-clad contracts
  and money in the bank! Patrons screaming in dark
  theaters! Ticket holders standing in long lines! Grip Boys
  auditioning in cloakrooms!
Universal! Universal! Nightmare of Universal! Universal the
  calculating! Ravenous Universal! Universal the devourer
  of thespians!
Universal the slaughterhouse of essence! Universal the
  flesh-grinding boneless junkyard and Studio of
  terror! Universal whose films are USDA graded!
  Universal the meat cleaver of inspection! Universal
  the concrete productions!
Universal whose checkbook is bottom line! Universal whose

life is zombie profit! Universal whose thoughts
are small implosions! Universal whose head is a cannabis
fire pit! Universal whose heart is a ticking bomb!
Universal whose eyes are a thousand blank expressions!
Universal whose runaway success litters the crowded
theaters like recycled storylines! Universal whose king-
pins burn angry torches in boardrooms! Universal whose
castles are ablaze in production codes!
Universal whose desire is countless cash and decay! Universal
whose hunchback soul is mayhem and madness! Universal
whose existence is a suspension of belief! Universal
whose face is a Frankenstein of tortuous makeup!
Universal whose name is the Horror!
Universal in whom I drink alone! Universal in whom I cast out
Demons! Revulsion in Universal! Repulsion in
Universal! Fanged and hairy in Universal!
Universal who signed me on the dotted line! Universal in whom
I am an image flickering without a light! Universal
who drank me stumbling under the table! Universal
whom I surrender to! Make me over in Universal!
Darkness creeping into all my best scenes!
Universal! Universal! Moaning remakes! creaking sequels!
man made monsters! dead man's eyes! strange
confession! pillow of death! the mummy's tomb!
the mummy's ghost! the mummy's curse! monstrous
bombs!
They broke their sprit digging up bodies for Universal! Publicity
stunts, phony names, gossip, witch hunts, done! burying
the past in the present for a future that doesn't exist
and is nowhere to be found!
Television! rights! syndication! series! episodes!
vanished in the weekly American ether!
Breakdowns! beyond the studio! flops and flashes of brilliance
gone! second chance! agents! schedule of guest
appearances! over the top! reality takes and fantasy
retakes! can't remember! another drink to forget! break
later! Sixty-five years' animal prayers and murders!
Unreal Hollywood howls in the night! They saw it coming! the
feral creatures! the Hollywood hounds! They leapt and
bound! They threw themselves off towers! to grief!
gesturing! swinging silver canes! Down to the studio!
onto the screen!

III.

Larry Talbot! I'm with you in Llanwelly
where you're prouder than I am

I'm with you in Llanwelly
    where you must pretend you cannot die
I'm with you in Llanwelly
    where you mimic the phantom of my opera
I'm with you in Llanwelly
    where you've killed your chance for an Oscar
I'm with you in Llanwelly
    where you mock the screams of your victims
I'm with you in Llanwelly
    where we both miss our marks in the same scenes
    with the Invisible Man
I'm with you in Llanwelly
    where your movies have become classics and
    are reviewed favorably in all the trades
I'm with you in Llanwelly
    where the lines of the script do not match
    the alcohol of tormented speech
I'm with you in Llanwelly
    where you drink the blood of the priest of the
    church of the son of Dracula
I'm with you in Llanwelly
    where you weep into the reels of your box office
    victories of the last one hundred years
I'm with you in Llanwelly
    where your face takes six hours to apply
    and three hours to remove in 17 shots
    of continuous dissolve
I'm with you in Llanwelly
    where the beast eye searches the stars with
    looks so close you can touch Evelyn Ankers
    in a gloomy trance of moody romance
I'm with you in Llanwelly
    where fifty thousand dollars will guarantee your
    next starring role in a breakout part in another
    familiar nightmare brought in under budget
I'm with you in Llanwelly
    where you charge your friends with complicity
    and tear up the lamented contracts nailed to
    your dressing room door
I'm with you in Llanwelly
    where you will split the proceeds of your final return
    and resurrect Abbott and Costello from the
    ashcan of second-rate comedians
I'm with you in Llanwelly
    where there are thousands of child actors in chorus lines
    all at once baying the dirge of death
I'm with you in Llanwelly

where we embrace the extension of our personality
of strange mortal men on the cutting room floor
who shriek all night and won't let us dream
I'm with you in Llanwelly
where we stalk the spotlight crisscrossing the dreary
sky heavy drinking waiting to enter and hear be told,
O even a man who is pure in heart
and says his prayers by night may become a wolf
when the wolfbane blooms and the autumn moon is bright,
O hulking bulk of mutton and corn O lump of alcoholic
clay O massive wreck of suffering bone O friend
remove your makeup we're free
I'm with you in Llanwelly
in my perfect rewrite you escape your part from a closed
set flee across a backlot of movie screens in triumph
to the door of my father's crypt in the Hollywood night.

-- -- --

Footnote To Howl Of Lon Chaney, Jr.

Hollywood! Hollywood! Hollywood! Hollywood! Hollywood!
Hollywood! Hollywood! Hollywood! Hollywood!
Hollywood! Hollywood! Hollywood! Hollywood!
Hollywood! Hollywood!
The word is hollywood! The script is hollywood!
The film is hollywood! The sound is hollywood!
The lighting and costumes and sets
and direction hollywood!
Everything is hollywood! everybody's hollywood! everywhere is
hollywood! everyday is on location! Everyone's
a film star!
The leading man's as hollywood as the prop man!
The performance is hollywood as you my portrayals
are hollywood!
The script change is hollywood the dialogue is hollywood
the direction is hollywood the moviegoers are
hollywood the experience is hollywood!
Hollywood Evelyn hollywood Lon hollywood Bela hollywood
Boris hollywood Carradine Hollywood Lorre hollywood
Price hollywood Lanchester hollywood the unbilled
player and anguished extra hollywood the hopeless
ham actors!
Hollywood my mother in the wings! Hollywood
my silent cocksure father laugh clown laugh!
Hollywood the soaring soundtrack! Hollywood the only
show on ice. Hollywood the parties amphetamine

wannabes smoke & booze & blow!
Hollywood the refuge of thugs and rascals! Hollywood
       the hotels overbooked with the anxious! Hollywood
       the 70 mm cameras keep rolling after the final take!
Hollywood the closeup night on the town!
       Hollywood the wide angle love affair!
       Hollywood the drunken talent agents of desperation!
       Who thinks the San Fernando Valley IS
       the San Fernando Valley!
Hollywood Oklahoma City Hollywood Universal City Mapleton
       & Goldstadt Hollywood Colton Hollywood Transylvania
       Hollywood New Orleans Hollywood San Clemente!
Hollywood montage in deep focus Hollywood deep focus
       in montage hollywood the sign on the hill hollywood
       the flash frame hollywood the fifth of bourbon
       hollywood the Christ in Universal!
Hollywood the key hollywood the locket hollywood
       the dinner party hollywood the major and the minor
       hollywood the delusional tremors hollywood the sound
       hollywood the fury hollywood the special effects
       that signify nothing!
Hollywood kindness! human! friend! love! Hollywood! Mine!
       spirit! release! free will!
Hollywood the silver bullet heartbreaking tear-jerking ill-fated
       deadly envelope please of the heart!

3. The Reason I Am Here

GOD COMMANDS KATE SMITH
TO STOP SINGING THAT SONG

That's it. Put a lid on it.

I hear that song one more time
and I swear I start sending plagues.

God bless America my ass.
What the hell is wrong with you people?

RETURN WITH US NOW
TO THOSE THRILLING DAYS OF YESTERYEAR

Barely in my teens far from my home
I study for the priesthood at a Catholic seminary
and begin to itch and scratch in places
I know little about.

A doctor in town prescribes an ointment
tells me to apply it twice a day
sends it to the infirmary for me to pick up
jokes about boys being boys.

That evening during study hall
a priest who expels boys for talking back
summons me to his bedroom
tells me my medical problem is now his.

For months everything he says and does to me
grows more and more weary and mysterious
each visit preceded and followed
by prayers invoking our lord and savior.

One night my body springs from his mouth
slips through his hands leaps from his bed
and races round and round the room
as music from a phonograph down the hall
plays the William Tell overture.

O, how I laugh inside at the sight
of all those sidekick angels hovering above
chasing after me whooping and hollering
kicking their spotted palominos.

Out in front on a white stallion is Jesus in a mask.
Like a cloud of dust and song
he gallops in the lead to head me off at the pass.

The Three Stooges
get an invitation
to a big party
at John Wayne's house
but besides the Stooges
the only people
who show up are
Randolph Scott
Stuart Whitman
and Glen Campbell
who all drop acid
and beat the shit
out of John Wayne
just for the hell of it

John Wayne looks
to the Stooges for help
but they're too busy
melting down his Oscar

THE PEACH SEED MAN

A FOUND POEM / ROBIN WILLIAMS: THE PLAYBOY INTERVIEW, 1992

I.

Jerzy Kosinski killed himself.
The reason was that he didn't want to lose his sharpness.

There's that fear.
If I felt like I was becoming not just dull but a rock,

that I still couldn't spark,
still fire off or talk about things,

if I'd start to worry
or got too afraid to say something.

If I stop trying, I'd get afraid.

So it was fear.
Now I'm not afraid.

II.

It isn't because of the drugs or anything.

I didn't read most interviews
for fear of having said something strange
or having stepped in a hole.

It's like jerking off in a wind tunnel.
Whoosh!—it blows back in your face!

After a while I felt I should have gone:

"Ladies and gentlemen,
let my dick speak for himself:

I love the guy
and when he's not choking me
he's a fabulous person."

You basically get where your eyes dim
and the world seems all right

and you kind of tighten up so much

that your sphincter doesn't open.
I don't want to deny life to anybody,
but sometimes you have to choose,

and it's a horrible choice, I'm not denying that.

Whatever strap-on attachment you use,
you still look like a poodle
and someone has to get a fire hose.

III.

I was not suicidal, but fucked up.

I was just out of my fucking mind.
I was totally out of control.

It was either fear
or just a sheer wanting to run away from it all.

I couldn't imagine
living the way I used to live.

I don't remember it as being anything
except quick, with this series of people

flashing through my life.

Here's this guy
who could do anything, and he's gone.

That sobered the shit out of everybody.

IV.

I don't want to take anybody else's time.

Every person is driven
by some deep, deep secret,
and finding it drives you through.

Sometimes you want to keep people
at a distance, people who have had four cocktails,
twelve beers, going, "Blow me!"

Do you really want to let them in?
"Come, let me share with you my deepest secrets."

But you should be careful,
because you might start talking about something
you're not ready to deal with.

Some issues are deeply personal.
I get near them and think,
I'm not ready to deal with that yet.

When you're comfortable with it,
you can be free about it.
If not, it's open-heart surgery.

It's a voice that tells you: danger.
They just want to see you drop.

Kill the comic, flatten the boy.
Watch the little furry guy go down.

It's like comedy terrorism.
It's getting near the edges of people's credulity,

where you start to fuck with the premise
of what they hold near and dear.

Nothing there. What do you do?
Oh, God, the great abyss.

If you take the chance,
sometimes you'll find something so magnificent
that it was worth dying for.

V.

I had a wonderful childhood.
I just made this incredible fantasy life
because I had only myself to play with.

My most precious object
is a thing my father gave me.

A little carved netsuke called a Peach Seed Man.
It's a little boy popping out of a peach seed.

When my dad gave it to me
a couple weeks before he died, he said:

"This is you."

A hydrogen bond is a true bond.
So is Roger Moore.

A two-by-four is 2 inches by 4 inches.
Al Capone was in the insurance business.

Peanuts are nuts.
Everyone in my mother's family is not.

The American buffalo is a buffalo.
Chief Joseph agreed to live on a reservation.

A koala bear is a bear.
Yogi Berra was manager of the Cubs.

Swollen glands are glands.
My father always used a condom.

A starfish is a fish.
Arnold Schwarzenegger is an actor.

It costs one cent to make two pennies.
It took two years to write this one line.

A palm tree is a tree.
I think that I shall never see one.

The Boy Who Slept with a Bowling Ball

In junior high school I knew a sweet but awkward kid
who apparently slept with a bowling ball.

We weren't close friends but I think we wanted something
from each other that neither of us knew how to give.

We hung out a few times after school
mostly because I needed an excuse not to go home.

One day I went over to his house
to listen to 45s on his portable record player

and saw this big, round lump under the blankets on his bed.
"That's my bowling ball," he said acting cool,

which was weird since he was anything but cool.
He told me he gave his bowling ball a name,

a common boy's name, something like "Johnny" or "Bobby"
or "Jimmy" or maybe it was "Ralph,"

which wouldn't make much sense since that was *his* name.
But I can't remember for sure.

I think I blocked it from my memory
to keep from explaining how I really felt

sitting on his bedroom floor listening to Roger Miller
singing about trailers for sale or rent, midnight trains

and old stogies, short, but not too big around,
touching one another in places just beyond our reach.

Over the years I've tried to recall the name
of that bowling ball as if it would make any difference.

All I ever manage is a face, a soft, inquisitive face,
and me, wondering what it was like under those blankets,

to curl my body around something so smooth and hard,
to sleep with something cold enough to keep me warm.

KNOWING WHEN TO STAY DOWN

I idolize my older brother.
I adore him so much
he inspires me to construct
a small altar in our shared bedroom
a modest shrine to his many deeds:

A near-perfect report card
a third place track medal
a handwritten note
scribbled on a scrap of yellow paper
a dried white carnation
worn to a school dance
a black and white photograph
of him smiling back at me.

He says I'm weird
and he's right.

I'm a *Jordaniare* to his Elvis
thrilled to be standing
on the same stage with him.

He grows older handsomer
notices me less and less.

I pester him more and more
tunnel under his skin
mapping routes to his heart
where common bonds beg release.

Four years older six inches taller
in the basement one day fed up
he catches me with a roundhouse
knocks me flat on my ass.

I get right back up
make silly noises
hop around in loopy circles
like Daffy Duck.

He knocks me down again
I pop right back up again
dancing and prancing
until he screams at me to stay down.

Then he hauls off and nails me
like a head-on collision.

I drop to my knees this time
see green and gold fairies
sit there dazed
try to shake it off
buy some time

I don't let on how it hurts
how I muster all my courage
not to rub my face
not to cry
not to run off
and scream at him all
the dirty words he's taught me.

I stare at the cement floor
catch my breath
and then it comes to me:

Is this yours? I ask
pick up a tiny speck of dirt
pretend to examine it closely

He can't resist his own curiosity
What is it? he demands
leaning in to get a closer look.

I think it's part of your brain I say
and offer it to him
in mock reverence
one hand raised up
like a gift at the altar rail
until both of us bust out laughing.

A soft light slices a small crack
in the basement door
and skips along a stream of dust
near my brother's face.

How good it feels
to know someone that well.

There is a chilly scuffle in the Chicago sky
a brisk sharp wind slicing off the lake.

Birds chipped grey with celluloid wings
race past in migratory speed
and whip it up like daily rushes
shot against a black and white tale
straight out of a John Ford film.

Corso lights another Pall Mall.
He blows smoke in his own face
does his best thinking
inside a swirling blue tobacco haze.

It's business as usual, he says.
Like some Medea in the nameless night
sleeping in the veins that bleeds our words
until all meaning is pale and still.

I have no idea what he's talking about.
I've been hopping up and down
on the same street corner for hours
listening to a ghost go on and on
about the end of something or other
and all I can think about
is how to keep from freezing to death.

He argues that Kerouac and Cassidy
got it right the first time
whatever that means
and that Ginsberg and Burroughs
and even Gary Snyder skipped a beat
when they thought they could sleep
with Bob Dylan.

What about Anne Waldman?
and Diane di Prima? I ask
tossing out these names
like so much kindling
with no idea how to contribute
to this one-sided conversation
but hoping to distract him long enough
to steal his matches.

To hear Corso tell it
we are forever joined at the hip
playing the final scene in *Casablanca*
where Humphrey Bogart
and Claude Rains walk off together
destined to go on fighting for just causes
even though it feels
more like Abbott and Costello
in *Waiting for Godot.*

Corso suddenly becomes enraged.
He starts shouting
as if we're in a prison movie
and this is the part where we bust out:
Free yourself, you fucking morons!
All the techno gods of your disconnected world
won't save you from staring into your hand!

I blow on my fingers
to keep them from breaking off.
I can't figure out
why he's so worked up.

I try to remember that he's dead
that I'm dying
that he isn't relevant
neither am I
that we don't belong here
that we have no business hanging around
that none of this
has anything to do with poetry
and why is it so goddamn cold?

Corso talks about hell freezing over
then squints and smiles
like Robert De Niro in *Taxi Driver.*
He stares at me as if he's looking into a mirror.
He pretends he's talking to himself
only he's talking to me
asking himself if I'm talking to me.

Then he shuts up. His jaw drops
and I watch his screwy eyes trace the path
of escaping birds above our heads,
notice how he waits for something
watching for anything
to just happen.

Inhaling the smoke
from one cigarette after another
he exhales slowly.
Savoring the smugness of a voice
borrowed from Clint Eastwood
he looks me in the eye and says:
Go ahead, make my day.

I don't have time.
An icy wind is howling off the frozen lake
and I can't feel my toes.

ZORRO CARVES A "Z"
IN THE BACK OF BONO'S HEAD
WHEN THE SINGER IS TEN YEARS OLD

As Tyrone Power
I held a razor to my own throat.

Stick with me kid and someday you too
will have the edge.

On the first channel
Burt Lancaster is preaching
to a tent full of Holy Rollers
and smiling through a mouth full of teeth.

On the second channel
a Sunday football game
is dropped behind the line of scrimmage
and there are no more timeouts.

I surf between the two
and keep the TV on mute
holy and respectful
like being in church.

The quarterback scrambles
in blessed silence
tossing *Hail Mary* bombs
beyond the outreached hands
of intended receivers
as incomplete prayers explode
without a sound.

Lancaster is brilliant.
He stares right into the camera
and dares me to ignore his performance
begs me to read his lips:
How many folks have got the guts
to play on God's team?

I turn on the radio.
A panel of Sunday religion experts
debate the presence of God
in a secular society
as if there's a sacred need
to know what we don't believe in
and why it should matter.

Between Burt and the bouncing ball
only three religions
claim God exists:
Judaism, Christianity and Islam.
All the rest
are just fighting to maintain
a level playing field.

The Hollywood Catechism

poems

PAUL FERICANO

The Hollywood Catechism
poems
PAUL FERICANO

In **The Hollywood Catechism,** his latest collection of poems from Silver Birch Press of Los Angeles, Paul Fericano shines a bright searchlight on our addiction to pop culture, our fixation on celebrity worship and our suspicion of religious ideas. Fericano's unique perspective is marked by a skill and talent that blends socio-political satire with suffering and sentiment. In the process, he manages to acknowledge our shenanigans and celebrate our humanity.

"Paul Fericano is that rare poet who tells the truth with a laugh."
The San Francisco Chronicle

$16.00 • Free Shipping on Mail Orders
Paperback • 110 pages • 6 x 0.2 x 9

Check or Money Order Payable to:
Silver Birch Press • Box 29458 • Los Angeles. CA 90029
Or Order Via PayPal at: silverbirchpress@yahoo.com

Also Available Online at Amazon.com
Search Title: "The Hollywood Catechism"

SILVER BIRCH PRESS
LOS ANGELES, CALIFORNIA

I listen and stare at the screen.

The game is all about possession.
It has everything to do
with moving the ball downfield
and running out the clock.

Some sit in sky boxes
and call in all the plays.
Others watch from the sidelines
and repeat what they hear.
A few even claim to know
the secret to winning.

The rest of the faithful
show up year after year
despite a lifetime of losing seasons.
They tackle
and get tackled
and do their best
to recover the fumbles.

Faith requires sacrifice
but some play without a helmet
or even a ball.
Others drink their way
into a huddle until their fists
miss the point of intoxication.

Dozens of penalty flags
litter the field
Seconds tick away
like missed field goals
Millions start to check
the point spread
and everyone keeps looking
for God to get open in the end zone.

Lancaster knows the score.
Smiling, he holds a bible in one hand
and points to it.

None of this makes any sense
until baseball season starts.

ODE TO HENNY YOUNGMAN

Take my poem, please.

First Interview / October 15, 1984

Me: Mr. Miller, my name is . . .
Miller: Fuck you *(laughs)*.
Me: Excuse me?
Miller: Excuse you and fuck you *(laughs)*.

Second Interview / June 17, 1996

Me: Thanks for seeing me, Mr. Miller.
Miller: Go fuck yourself *(laughs)*.
Me: I believe we spoke on the phone?
Miller: Fuck off *(laughs)*.
Me: I don't understand.
Miller: Read a book and fuck you *(laughs)*.

Third Interview / March 19, 2001

Me: Mr. Miller?
Miller: Fuck you *(laughs)*.
Me. Mr. Miller?
Miller: Fuck you *(laughs)*.
Me: Mr. Miller?
Miller: Fuck you *(laughs)*.

Fourth Interview / August 21, 2008

Me. Mr. Miller, I spoke with your agent and he says . . .
Miller: Fuck you *(laughs)*.
Me: No, he says...
Miller: Fuck you *(laughs)*.
Me: No, really, he says . . .
Miller: Fuck you *(laughs)*.

Final Interview / January 23, 2015

Me: Mr. Miller?
Miller: Fuck off *(laughs)*.
Me: Mr. Miller?
Miller: Fuck off *(laughs)*.
Me. Mr. Miller?
Miller: What the fuck is your problem?

SHOOT ALL THE BLUEJAYS YOU WANT

At two o'clock in the morning
I'm awakened
by the clear distinct ringing of a cell phone
coming from somewhere
just outside my window.

A few low-quality beeps at first
then a high fidelity blast
of flawless imitations
performed in quick succession:

a bark
a bell tower
a cricket
a doorbell
a duck
a harp
a motorcycle
an old car horn
a piano riff
a pinball

Ending with a familiar little jingle
that rings and rings and rings

Until I realize
that what I'm listening to now
is the *iPhone's* irritating
18-note marimba default ring-tone

Over and over and over again

When suddenly
somewhere in the telltale dark of night
pleading and beseeching
I hear a neighbor's weak but desperate
cry for help:

For Christ's sake answer your goddamn phone!

And just like that
a mockingbird puts itself on *vibrate*

JOE DiMAGGIO EXPLAINS WHERE HE HAS GONE

I.

All this talk this singsong talk
about where I've gone
makes me shake my head
like a rosin bag
makes me wonder
if anyone ever listens ever watches
ever understands this game.

When I'm hot
when I'm really on fire
every ball I hit drops safely
impossibly
onto an unprotected patch of outfield grass
or scorches a hole
through an infield crack
of undefended dirt.

Some call it ability
others call it destiny
I only know
that when my hands feel the sting
of each swing as I make contact
there is no bat no ball no me
no nothing at all.

II.

Moments before
I kneel in the on-deck circle
waiting my turn
for what seems like a season
the roar from the stadium
recedes to the back of my head.

Like the volume on a radio
slowly being turned down
all I hear all I want to hear
is a familiar voice
from one of her films
a breathy voice that whispers low:
Come home, Joe, come home.

III.

When she says she loves me
my suspicions ignore her needs
my impatience swings
at everything she throws my way
especially herself
desirable and imperfect
unacceptable as she is
until the hits don't come so easily.

Her tears are like a rain delay
they wash away my hitting streak
like the allusion it becomes
I disappear like a foul ball
sliced into the stands
and just like that
I go from 56 straight
to 0 for 4
a feeling of relief
a mission of mercy to the mound.

IV.

What follows me from then on
moves so imperceptibly
it feels like grief
not mine but someone else's:
an infield pop-up
hitting into a double play
a slow dribbler down the first base line
a strikeout looking
in my final at bat.

I kick the dirt back to the dugout
I study the ground
with each measured step
I shun eye contact
with dumb determination
I tip my hat to the fans
feeling their disappointment
trailing behind me.

V.

In spite of a lifetime
of surprising skills
and multiple errors
I take the field a fortunate man
her simple desire to be held
her lucky embrace
the only play that matters
the only call that has a chance
of ever going my way.

See how I make the crowd believe
I play to win
watch how easily I hit one in the gap
steal a base
circle under a ball.

Look at me
jogging in when the game is over
when the score is added up.

What difference does it make
whose side I'm on?
what does it matter
where I have gone?

Isn't it enough that I am here?

THE POET LOSES HIS NERVE
AND RETHINKS FUNNY

This is that uncertain time
that anxious moment in the process
a point somewhere between TV and despair
when you stop writing
and your hands fall to your side
and you cock your head
and you listen

There it is again.

You recognize the sound:
the broken leg of a John Ashbery poem
the black eye of a Lenny Bruce routine
the missing thumb of a Harold Lloyd film

You sense the hum in your modifiers
a kind of electric surge
poised to jumpstart a muse
begging to be worthy
of all the trouble you try to hide from.

Wait a minute
don't move
stay very still.

Is that a puddle you're standing in?

MOTHER MAY I

Mother, may I
sit beside you
on the green mohair couch

late at night
like a wakeful dreamer
and watch old movies

on the black-and-white
television set
with bent rabbit ears

and rest awhile
near your soft and gentle heart
until I fall asleep?

Yes, you may

Mother, may I
light your menthol cigarettes
with the brushed chrome

cigarette lighter
that father gave you
on your first wedding anniversary

and marvel as the smoke rings
float like halos
just above your head?

Yes, you may

Mother, may I
tell the woeful stories
you tried to tell

of love gone bad
that left you alone
to live this stubborn life?

No, you may not

but you may
take three steps backward
and finish this poem

When our mother and father fight it's always
a mystery. We never know what hits us.
We run for cover pissing in our pants
trying to escape the sledgehammer blows
of their misdirected lunacy.

The Three Stooges are different.
Their insanity is an inspiration.
They encourage me and my brothers to seek perfection;
to imitate lamebrains, numskulls and morons
as we climb trees and fall out of them on purpose.

Parents don't understand this, least of all ours.
They scream at us to grow up and behave.
They beat us with wooden spoons and leather belts.
They wish upon distant blue stars
for real boys to become *pinocchios*.

We don't care much for puppets who dream
of being us. No matter how we dance around
on bathroom tiles to escape the blows
we never get it through our thick wooden skulls.

We are betting boys.
Our money is on the three grown men
with strange haircuts who never grow up.
When we dream we dream of being them.

We struggle to be idiots. We practice
confusion, misunderstanding and sheer stupidity.
If there are mistakes worth repeating
these are the lessons committed to memory:

how to fall down and spin like human buzz saws;
how to bark like mournful dogs and chase after cars;
how to heave dirt clods at each other and marvel
at the huge chunks of clay and rock that literally
bounce off our happy heads.

Later and with whatever good sense we have left
we rush inside each day exactly at four o'clock
turn the TV set on, hold our breath
and watch how the experts do it.

SINATRA, SINATRA

Sexual reference:
A protruding sinatra
is often laughed at by serious women.

Medical procedure:
A malignant sinatra
must be cut out by a skilled surgeon.

Violent persuasion:
A sawed-off sinatra
is a dangerous weapon at close range.

Congressional question:
Do you deny the charge of ever being
involved in organized sinatra?

Prepared statement:
Kiss my sinatra.
Blow it out your sinatra.

Financial question:
Will supply-side sinatra halt inflation?

Empty expression:
The sinatra stops here.
The sinatra is quicker than the eye.

Strategic question:
Do you think it's possible to win
a limited nuclear sinatra?

Stupid assertion:
Eat sinatra.
Hail Mary full of sinatra.

Serious reflection:
Sinatra this, sinatra that.
Sinatra do, sinatra don't.
Sinatra come, sinatra go.
There's no sinatra like show sinatra.

Historical question:
Is the poet who wrote this poem still alive?

Biblical fact:
Man does not live by sinatra alone.

STOOGISM

i dreamt of Moe
last night
he was crying
he took
the laughter
out of his head
and thanked me
and when I saw
myself
about to cry
he whispered:
wake up
and go to sleep
and i did

THE BOY IN THE RED CHEVROLET

I.

I didn't know his real name and even pretended
he didn't have one and liked that so much better.

Every morning he'd stare out the window
from the back seat of his father's bright red Chevy Bel Air
as it glided past our house on Teddy Avenue
in San Francisco.

We made eye contact once until I realized
it was just my own reflection in my bedroom window
watching him disappear down the street.

I imagined his good fortune satisfied just to think
this lucky boy no older than me
was going somewhere anywhere in that red Chevrolet.

A boy who didn't have to answer to any name at all
who was being driven someplace in a red car
a cool red car that Dinah Shore sang about on TV.

II.

I was lucky if I remembered my own name
without saying it out loud.

I lived in a house lumped in with eleven other siblings
bumping up against each other constantly being mistaken
for someone else by mothers, fathers, aunts, uncles,
cousins and even one another.

We wandered among the self the hopeless few lost
in the uneasy mix of guess-who covered in doubtful recognition.

Olive-skinned refugees from a foreign house
with dark-haired names pulled down over our faces
like old hats worn by shadowy immigrants off the boat:

Salvatore, Josefina, Paolo, Anna Maria
Antonio, Giuseppe, Francesca, Francesco
Annucia, Teresa, Giovanni Valentino

and *Maria Rosa Eva Isabella Giralda* our youngest sister
whose name paid tribute to my mother's four sisters
and St. Gerard the patron saint of expectant mothers
unborn children and the falsely accused.

III.

The adults were amused as if it were a game of pinochle
where everyone showed their hand at once
names being rattled off without warning one after another
in quick succession like a litany of mournful souls
trapped in purgatory.

Most of us learned to speak up right away without thinking
take our chances answer to anything even *"che fai!"*
and stand there like a mystery guest on *I've Got A Secret.*

Some of us mindful of the fragile uncertainty
of our own suspicions stayed quiet and remembered
all that chrome and two-tone hardtop convertible speed
that took us away to see the USA in our Chevrolet.

SHERLOCK HOLMES GETS MELANCHOLY
WHILE TAKING OFF HIS SHOES

See that heel?
I ran that down.

MY STEREOTYPE LIFE AS A MIDDLE CHILD

I am the thin slice of neglected baloney
Stuck between two wedges of *Wonder* bread

The tossed banana peel no one slips on
The plain birthday cake in a pink cardboard box

The extra syllable of a pointless word
The curse spoken in jest and reduced to slang

I am the easygoing boy who lacks friends
The dreamer, the artist, the player of trombones

Harmonicas and upright pianos with missing keys
The scribbler and doodler on wide-ruled paper

The digger of holes in dirt clod backyards
The loner who can't maintain a career

I am the hidden bald spot of a butch haircut
The careless promise of a bowl of cherries

The forgotten date on a calendar by the bed
The missed opportunity of a drawn-out afternoon

The ordinary pair of hand-me-down shoes
The brown tweed coat too big for baby

There are reasons to instigate and misbehave
To be secretive and work as little as possible

To seek out and be envious of winning leaders,
Presidents, baseball players, chiropractors,

Grocery clerks, dentists, yoga instructors,
Bicycle repairmen, spirit guides and more

There is cause to be fair and just in the middle
In the center of everything that doesn't move

FROG HAIKU
BY MATSUO BASHO

Translation by Porky Pig

Into the quiet of the primor-mor, the pri-m-m-mor—
er, the very old pond
the small f-f-fr-, the small f-f-f-fr—
er, the toad leaps.
The water sound is b-b-beau-, b-b-beau-, b-b—
oh, never mind.

When Everything Is Said and Done

I.

I'm not a guy who goes looking for trouble
I only fight the current if I'm too far downstream

Even as a kid when it was three against one
I never ran from a fair fight

I was small but wiry and pounced on bullies
who taunted my sisters and slapped them around

II.

When everything is said and done
There's no easy way to come from behind

I stop in the middle where so much of me
Is ground to the bone not because I mean to

But because getting beat never comes close
To how desperately I pretend to be unbeatable

III.

A motel owner insulted my mother once
He said she cleaned toilets like she never used one

I was just one number away from Vietnam
When I burst through the door and grabbed his throat

Afterwards he threatened to call the police
I grabbed his throat again and handed him the phone

IV.

In the silent film *Steamboat Bill, Jr.*
A cyclone hits the town as Buster Keaton struggles

to walk against the wind before he's finally blown
down the street through the mud on his face in one take

The fact that he eventually rescues both his father
and the woman he loves is beside the point

THE YEAR IN REVIEW

My father sits in his favorite *La-Z-Boy* recliner
and watches reruns of *McHale's Navy* on TV.
He is barely able to breathe.

In between the commercials
he tells off-color jokes and plays a few hands
of five card draw with his hospice nurse.

My mother is dying in the next room.
She prays the rosary for the second time that day
and prefers her own set of sorrowful mysteries.

Two *Hail Marys* into the third decade she screams:
I hate the sound of that man's voice!
with words cold and hard as the beads she fingers.

My father doesn't wonder too much about this.
He slowly wets his lips with his tongue
and thinks she's talking about Ernest Borgnine.

THE REASON I AM HERE

A slim book of my poems,
a first collection
published in 1977,
hides its face on a shelf
in the poetry section
of the local library in town.

Gathering the dust
of its own vague history
it anticipates readers
the same way a blind beggar
listens for footsteps.

I am in a tight spot but good company.

I am neatly wedged
between Robert Fergusson
and Lawrence Ferlinghetti.

Fergusson,
an eighteenth century
Scottish poet,
was an influence on Robert Burns.

Dead and buried for two centuries
he is borrowed regularly,
twice this month, in fact,
and as recently as yesterday.

Ferlinghetti, still with us at 95
is, after all, Ferlinghetti.

He flies off the shelf
so often and so fast
that I am frequently seen
leaning on Edward Field
awkwardly but lovingly
for much of the year.

Visitors can't understand it.
What are you doing here? they ask.

I am waiting, I tell them,
for someone to check me out.

PRAYER OF THE TALKING HEAD

Lord, make me an instrument of my baloney;
Where there is truth, let me speak hokum;
where there is logic, twaddle;
where there is fact, drivel;
where there is sense, gabble;
where there is intellect, bunkum;
and where there is reason, mumbo jumbo.

O Divine Master,
grant that I may not so much speak
to be flabbergasted, as to flabbergast;
to be flummoxed, as to flummox;
to be flimflammed, as to flimflam.
For it is in jabbering that we jabber,
it is in blabbering that we are blabbered,
and it is in gibberish that we are born to eternal hooey.

MOREY BE

Morey be to the Amsterdam,
and to the Dick,
and to the Mary Tyler Moore.
As it was in the ratings,
is now, and ever shall be,
TV without Rose Marie.
Amen.

NOTES

"The Actor's Creed": Although there is still some disagreement over religious interpretation of the selection process following the death of Judas Iscariot, most biblical scholars generally acknowledge that Mathias was chosen to become the thirteenth apostle.

"Dean Martin Talks About What's Bothering Him": *Coulomb's Law* is the fundamental law of electrostatics stating that the force between two charged particles is directly proportional to the product of their charges and inversely proportional to the square of the distance between them.

"A Direct Correlation Between the War on Terror and the Proliferation of Penis Enlargement Spam": In *The Grand Piano,* the poetic application of justice or due process, especially at the level of sentencing, is the basic tenet of language praxis as applied to the polemics and theoretical documents of Barrett Watten, Lyn Hejinian, and Conrad Veidt.

"My Life In A Coma": In 1961, Mrs. McBain taught fifth grade at Southwood Junior High School in South San Francisco, California. She lasted one year. In 1962, the school district eliminated the grade and Mrs. McBain disappeared.

"I Don't Care If I Never Get Back": Ethel Merman and the author were both born on the same day (January 16).

"The Three Stooges Meet Charles Bukowski in Heaven": Jesus of Nazareth was crucified by the Romans on Golgotha (near Jerusalem) wearing only his underpants.

"Thank You Elizabeth Taylor": The song "Suicide Is Painless" was written by Johnny Mandel and Mike Altman in 1969.

"The Halle Berry": *Jockey* is a popular brand of underwear worn exclusively by jockeys.

"Thirteen Ways of Looking at a Black Man": When dining out, Wallace Stevens usually preferred Neapolitan ice cream for dessert.

"Poem For Ralph Edwards": This is his note.

"Father Writes to Ann Landers and Looks for Practical Guidance": Ann Landers wrote a bestseller, *Ann Landers Talks To Teen-Agers About Sex (1963),* which the author regrets never having read as a teenager.

"A Beautiful Day in the Neighborhood": Gordon McRae served as a navigator in the United States Army Air Force during World War II.

"Howl Of Lon Chaney, Jr.": At the American Library Association Book Fair held in San Francisco in 1978, Allen Ginsberg visited the author's table and spent time thumbing through a copy of *Stoogism Anthology.* He eventually bought the book for five dollars and remarked afterwards: "Stoogism is the only movement with a punch line."

"The Peach Seed Man": Robin Williams (1951 – 2014).

"Return with Us Now to Those Thrilling Days of Yesteryear": William Tell is the former rhythm guitarist for the piano rock band *Something Corporate.*

"The Hollywood Catechism" quotes Spinoza's *Ethics,* Part III, Prop. 59, as translated by Edwin Curley (Penguin Classics), and draws on C.S. Lewis's chapter "Time and Beyond Time" from *Mere Christianity* (Harper-Collins).

"Ode To Henny Youngman": In 1975, William F. Buckley mistook Rodney Dangerfield for Jackie Vernon, who once opened for Steve Lawrence and Eydie Gormé.

"The Dennis Miller Interviews": Marion is a city of Northeast-Central Indiana. A marionette is a jointed puppet manipulated from above by strings or wires attached to its limbs.

"Sinatra, Sinatra": Social psychiatry is the branch of psychiatry that deals with the relationship between social environment and mental illness. A pip is a dot indicating a unity of numerical value on dice. An iamb is a metrical foot used in various types of poetry.

"Sherlock Holmes Gets Melancholy While Taking Off His Shoes": Men's full brogue Oxford dress (size 10 ½).

"Frog Haiku": The former Zellerbach paper plant just off Spruce Avenue in South San Francisco, California, was once the site of a secret hideout used by Joaquín Murietta during the California gold rush.

"When Everything Is Said And Done": Most of the satires of Gaius Lucilius were written in hexameters, but, so far as an opinion can be formed from a number of unconnected fragments, he seems to have written the trochaic tetrameter with a smoothness, clearness, and simplicity which he never attained in handling the hexameter.

"Prayer of the Talking Head": Al Franken was right.

ACKNOWLEDGEMENTS

The author gratefully acknowledges the following publications where some of the poems in this book appeared in full or different form:

MAGAZINES, BROADSHEETS, AND ONLINE JOURNALS

The Antarctic Review, A Room With A Pew, Askew, The Broadsider, The Bubble, Covered Wagon, The Cane Toad Times (Australia), *Diario Catarinense* (Brazil), *The Dust Congress, El Espectador* (Colombia), *The Fault, Four By Two, Frankie, Haggard and Halloo, Heavy Bear, The Hilton Review, House Beautiful, Johnny Got His Gun, Le Fringe* (Paris), *Little City Review* (Berlin), *The Mas Tequila Review, Medusa's Kitchen, Minestrone, The Outlaw Poetry Network, The Oxford Journal of Poetry, The Parmesean Review, Poems For All, Poetry Now, Poets & Poetry* (Rome), *Projector, The James Remar Review* (Hong Kong), *Silver Birch Press, Star West, Stone Turntable, The Straits Times* (Singapore), *Tape Cop, The West Australian* (Perth), *The Wormwood Review, Yellow Brick Road.*

ANTHOLOGIES

A Bird Black as the Sun (Green Poet Press, 2011)

Bukowski: An Anthology of Poetry & Prose About Charles Bukowski (Silver Birch Press, 2013)

But Buddy I'm a Kind of Poem: A Sinatra Anthology (Entasis Press, 2008)

Corners of the Mouth: A Celebration of Thirty Years of the San Luis Obispo Poetry Festival (Deer Tree Press, 2014)

Italo-American Poets, a Bilingual Anthology (Carello Editore, Italy, 1985)

May Poetry Anthology (Silver Birch Press, 2014)

Swallow Dance: A Collection of Poetry Chapbooks (Silver Birch Press, 2014)

Swift et Voltaire: Examen Comparatif (Editions de L'oreille, France, 1990)

Tutti Stupi Frutti: La Poesia di Anti-Fascismo (Marco Citelli, Italy, 1978)

AUTHOR COLLECTIONS

Commercial Break (Poor Souls Press, 1982)

Loading the Revolver with Real Bullets (Second Coming Press, 1977)

ABOUT THE AUTHOR

Paul Fericano is a poet, satirist and social activist. He was born in San Francisco in 1951, the year the term "rock and roll" was first used on the radio. He is the editor and cofounder of *Yossarian Universal* (1980), the nation's first parody news service. Since 1971, his poetry and prose have appeared, disappeared, and reappeared in various underground and above-ground literary and media outlets in this country and abroad, including: *The Antarctic Review, Inside Joke, Mother Jones, New York Quarterly, Poetry Now, Projector, The Realist, Saturday Night Live, SoHo Arts Weekly, Vagabond, The Wormwood Review,* and *Catavencu Incomod* (Romania), *Charlie Hebdo* (Paris), *Il Male* (Italy), *Krokodil* (Moscow), *Pardon* (Germany), *Punch* (London), and *Satyrcón* (Argentina).

His chapbooks and books of poetry and fiction include: *Cancer Quiz* (Scarecrow Books, 1977), *Commercial Break* (Poor Souls Press, 1982), *The One Minute President (with Elio Ligi* / Stroessner Verlag, 1986), and *Interview with the Scalia* (Peabody Press, 1994). *Loading the Revolver with Real Bullets* (Second Coming Press, 1977), a collection of his work partly funded by the state of California, achieved notoriety in 1978, when one of its poems, "The Three Stooges at a Hollywood Party," was read on the floor of the California State Senate as a reason to abolish the California Arts Council.

In 1982, he received the *Howitzer Prize* for his poem, "Sinatra, Sinatra," an award he himself created and exposed as a literary hoax to reveal the absurd nature of competitive awards. The following year, *Commercial Break* received both the *Prix de Voltaire* (Paris) and the *Ambrose Bierce Prize* (San Francisco) for upholding the traditions of socio-political satire.

He currently serves as director of *Instruments of Peace/ SafeNet* (2003), a nonprofit reconciliation group for survivors of clergy sexual abuse and writes an online column on the healing process ("A Room With A Pew"). He is a resident of the San Francisco peninsula.

Author photo by Kate Kelly

Made in the USA
San Bernardino, CA
06 February 2016